Were They Real?

Written and illustrated by
Scoular Anderson

 Collins

Contents

Cleopatra

Cleopatra was queen of Egypt over two thousand years ago. She was very beautiful. The Romans won a battle against her army and put her in prison. Some say she used poison, hidden in a comb, to kill herself. Others say she was bitten by a snake.

Was she real?

There was a queen of Egypt called Cleopatra. Two great men fell in love with her. One was the Roman, Julius Caesar. The other was the general of her army, Mark Antony. He thought the Romans had killed her so he stabbed himself. When Cleopatra found out, she killed herself.

Boudica

Queen Boudica took her army to London to attack the mighty Romans. Boudica means "victory".

Was she real?

Yes!

Boudica was a **warrior** queen of the Iceni tribe.
The Romans attacked her army and killed her
husband. Boudica wanted to get her revenge.
So she attacked London. She **defeated**
the Roman army and set fire to the city.
Boudica and her army moved north, but she lost
the next battle. She didn't want to be captured,
so she killed herself by drinking poison.

King Arthur

There was once a sword stuck in a stone.
Any **knight** who could pull the sword from
the stone would become king. Many tried but
all failed – except one. His name was Arthur.

Was he real?

No...
but maybe yes

The sword was called Excalibur. Arthur's kingdom was called **Camelot**. Brave knights went there to sit with Arthur at a round table. This is all make-believe ... but there **was** a great king who won many battles in England about 1500 years ago. Could it have been the same King Arthur?

Robin Hood

Robin Hood's real name was Robert Fitzooth, Earl of Huntingdon. He was an **outlaw** who robbed the rich and gave to the poor. He lived in the middle of Sherwood Forest with his gang called the Merry Men.

Was he real?

The **legend** of Robin Hood began about 800 years ago when people sat round the fire and told stories. The stories of Robin Hood and his Merry Men were very popular. In the stories, Robin was always finding new ways to annoy his enemy, the Sheriff of Nottingham.

The Pied Piper

About 700 years ago there were thousands of rats in a town called Hamelin, in Germany. The people in the town promised to pay a piper if he got rid of the rats. The piper walked out of the town playing his pipe and the rats followed him and were never seen again.

Was he real?

No!

This is only a **legend**. In the legend, the people did not pay the piper, so the piper walked out of the town again, playing his pipe. This time, all the children in the town followed him and were never seen again. The word "pied" means "a mixture". The pied piper wore clothes with a mixture of colours.

Pocahontas

Pocahontas was the daughter of a Native American chief. Her father ordered that an Englishman called John Smith should be killed. Pocahontas jumped in front of John Smith before the braves could kill him with their spears.

Was she real?

After Pocahontas saved John Smith, they became very good friends. Pocahontas helped to bring peace between the Native Americans and the English who had come to live in America. Later, she married another Englishman called John Rolfe. They visited England together. Before they could return to America, Pocahontas became ill and died.

Blackbeard

Blackbeard was one of the fiercest pirates of all time. He looked scary. He had a long beard which he tied with ribbons. He always wore black clothes and kept daggers, **cutlasses** and pistols in his belt. (And, he also used bad language!)

Was he real?

Blackbeard's real name was Edward Teach.
He attacked so many ships that the king's navy
was sent to arrest him. Blackbeard fought
fiercely, even though he was badly wounded.
After he was killed, a total of 25 wounds were
found on his body.

Dracula

Count Dracula lived in a castle near a country called Transylvania (now part of Romania). He only went out at night. He was called a vampire because he crept into people's bedrooms and bit them in the neck with his sharp fangs.

Was he real?

No!

Dracula was a character in a book written by Bram Stoker more than 100 years ago. The author may have got the idea from another story about a king of Romania. This king was a very **bloodthirsty** man who called himself "Dracul".

Tarzan

Tarzan was an English gentleman whose real name was Lord Greystoke. When he was a baby, he went on a ship with his parents. The ship was wrecked near Africa. Baby Greystoke was found by chimpanzees who looked after him. Tarzan stayed in the jungle once he had grown up.

Was he real?

Tarzan was a character in some books written by the American author, Edgar Rice Burroughs. There are more than 40 Tarzan films and television series. Many different actors have played the part of Tarzan.

Index

Glossary

bloodthirsty	cruel, gruesome
braves	warriors of Native American tribes
Camelot	the place where people think King Arthur sat in court
cutlasses	short swords
defeated	beaten in battle
knight	a man – usually on horseback – who served a lord
legend	a popular story from long ago

outlaw   someone who breaks the law

Romania   a country in South East Europe

sheriff   someone who is supposed to keep the law

warrior   a fighter in a war

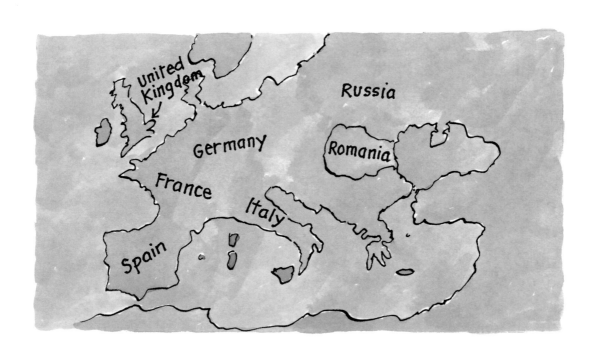

:paw: Ideas for guided reading :paw:

Learning objectives: use the structure of non-chronological reports to make predictions; evaluate how useful a text is for answering questions/for its purpose; know glossaries give definitions; collect new words from reading linked to topics; work in groups with each member taking a turn, challenging, supporting, moving.

Curriculum links: History: Why do we remember great people? How do we know about great events?

Interest words: thousand, beautiful, mighty, victory, captured, sword, make-believe, enemy, legend, peace, fiercely, wrecked

Word count: 843

Getting started

- Look at the front cover together and ask the children if they can name any of the people shown. Read the blurb on the back cover together. Discuss how some historical characters we think of as being real are actually fictional, and vice versa.
- Turn to the contents page (p2), and ask the children to use it to find Robin Hood in the book.
- Then ask them to look at the list of names on the contents page. Who have they heard of? Do they think these characters are real? Record their predictions.
- Skim through the book together, looking at the pictures and discussing the format: the right-hand page tells you about the character; the following left-hand page explains whether the character was real or not.

Reading and responding

- Ask the children to read silently and independently, observing each child and prompting and praising for self-correction and use of decoding strategies.
- Ask the children to look at their previous predictions about the characters and check how many they got right. Discuss.
- Turn to pp22-23, the illustrated glossary. Discuss the purpose of a glossary (to explain difficult or unusual words). Ask the children to pick a word from the glossary and find it in the book.